TALK LIKE A
BASKETBALL PLAYER

BY RYAN NAGELHOUT

 Gareth Stevens
PUBLISHING

Please visit our website, www.garethstevens.com. For a free color catalog of all our high-quality books, call toll free 1-800-542-2595 or fax 1-877-542-2596.

Cataloging-in-Publication Data

Names: Nagelhout, Ryan.
Title: Talk like a basketball player / Ryan Nagelhout.
Description: New York : Gareth Stevens, 2017. | Series: Let's talk sports! | Includes index.
Identifiers: ISBN 9781482456967 (pbk.) | ISBN 9781482456981 (library bound) | ISBN 9781482456974 (6 pack)
Subjects: LCSH: Basketball–Juvenile literature. | Basketball players–Juvenile literature.
Classification: LCC GV885.1 N34 2017 | DDC 796.323'64–dc23

First Edition

Published in 2017 by
Gareth Stevens Publishing
111 East 14th Street, Suite 349
New York, NY 10003

Copyright © 2017 Gareth Stevens Publishing

Designer: Samantha DeMartin
Editor: Ryan Nagelhout

Photo credits: Title art chudo-yudo/Shutterstock.com; series background Supphachai Salaeman/Shutterstock.com; cover, p. 1 inset Filipe Frazao/Shutterstock.com; cover, p. 1 basketball player Lopolo/Shutterstock.com; basketball caption Lightspring/Shutterstock.com; p. 4 Marcos Mesa Sam Wordley/Shutterstock.com; p. 5 eurobanks/Shutterstock.com; p. 6 prophoto14/Shutterstock.com; pp. 7, 11, 23 Kittichai/Shutterstock.com; p. 8 Brocreative/Shutterstock.com; p. 9 (main) Tom Herde/The Boston Globe/Getty Images; p. 9 (inset) Bronwyn Photo/Shutterstock.com; pp. 10, 25 Ezra Shaw/Getty Images Sport/Getty Images; p. 12 Greg Nelson/Sports Illustrated/Getty Images; p. 13 Nelson Marques/Shutterstock.com; pp. 14, 20 (bottom), 21 (both) Aspen Photo/Shutterstock.com; p. 15 Jason Miller/Getty Images Sport/Getty Images; p. 16 Joe Robbins/Getty Images Sport/Getty Images; p. 17 Heinz Kluetmeier/Sports Illustrated/Getty Images; p. 19 Paul Moseley/Fort Worth Star-Telegram/MCT via Getty Images; p. 20 (top) Pavel Shchegolev/Shutterstock.com; p. 24 Erik Drost/Wikimedia Commons; p. 26 Jeff Gross/Getty Images Sport/Getty Images; p. 27 JEWEL SAMAD/AFP/Getty Images; p. 29 (both) Halvorsen brian/Wikimedia Commons.

Printed in the United States of America

CPSIA compliance information: Batch #CW17GS : For further information contact Gareth Stevens, New York, New York at 1-800-542-2595.

CONTENTS

Words in the glossary appear in **bold** type the first time they are used in the text.

FOLLOW THE BOUNCES

Basketball is a game of **bounces**. And if you want to play, you need to know how to dribble. That's what basketball players call it when they bounce a basketball. Dribbling with your left and right hands, and maybe even between your legs, is an important skill for basketball players.

JAMES HARDEN

PLAYERS WHO ARE GOOD AT DRIBBLING ARE IMPORTANT MEMBERS OF A BASKETBALL TEAM.

LEARN THE LINGO

If you move with the ball and don't dribble, you get called for traveling! The other team is given the ball.

LET'S PLAY!

Dribbling is one of the most important parts of basketball. It's just one of the many terms we use to talk about the game. How much do you know about the sport? Let's find out!

◀ REFEREE SIGNALING TRAVELING

5

ON THE COURT

Before we start playing, let's learn some basics. The place you play basketball is called a court. Sometimes the court is inside a gymnasium, or gym. Basketball courts can also be found outside. **Professional** basketball courts are in big buildings called arenas!

BASKETBALL COURTS IN GYMS ARE MADE OF WOOD. THE COURT IN A GYM IS SOMETIMES CALLED THE "HARDWOOD."

OUT AND IN

Lines on the floor mark the court's shape. The two longer **parallel** lines are called the sidelines. The shorter parallel lines are called end lines. These four lines connect to create the floor.

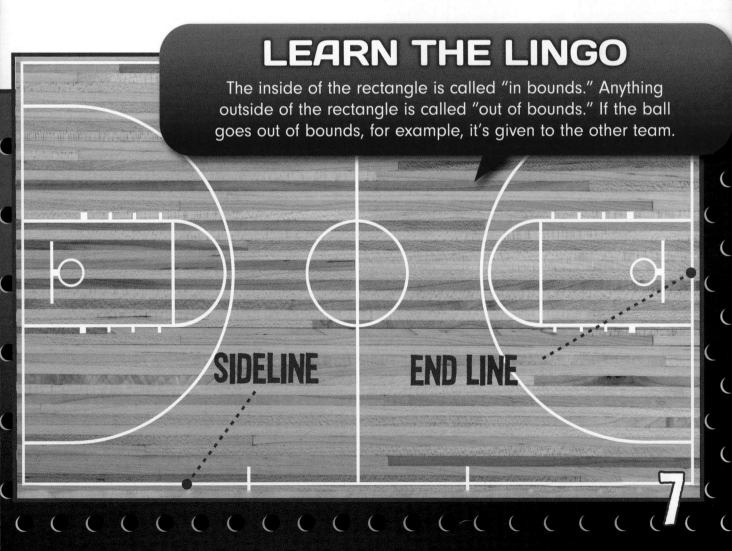

LEARN THE LINGO

The inside of the rectangle is called "in bounds." Anything outside of the rectangle is called "out of bounds." If the ball goes out of bounds, for example, it's given to the other team.

SIDELINE

END LINE

TO THE HOOP

Each basketball court has two rings called hoops. They hang above the court and parallel to it. Each hoop is connected to a flat surface called a backboard. In basketball, you want to shoot the ball through the hoop to score points.

BACKBOARDS USED BY *THE PROS* ARE CLEAR SO PEOPLE WATCHING IN THE STANDS CAN SEE *THROUGH THEM!*

PEACHES?

The first basketball hoops were peach baskets! Players had to use a ladder to get the ball out when they scored a "basket." Today's hoops are made of metal, with a net hanging under them to help you see if the ball went through the hoop.

LEARN THE LINGO

Some backboards are made of a kind of plastic you can see through. It's called plexiglass, which is why people call the backboard "the glass."

SCORING POINTS

The official name of a shot in basketball is a field goal. Basketball courts are often called the floor or field. When a player shoots and scores, where they are on the floor **determines** how much the basket is worth.

STEPHEN CURRY SHOOTS A 3-POINTER.

BOTH FEET NEED TO BE BEHIND THE ARC FOR IT TO BE A 3-POINTER. OTHERWISE, THE SHOT IS WORTH 2 POINTS.

TWO OR THREE?

The 3-point line is a line that forms a half circle, or arc, at a fixed length from the basket. A shot taken anywhere inside the 3-point line is a 2-point field goal. Any shot taken from beyond the line is worth 3 points!

3-POINT LINE

LEARN THE LINGO

Made shots in basketball are often called "buckets." There are also lots of names for a 3-point field goal. It's often called a "3-pointer" or a "trey."

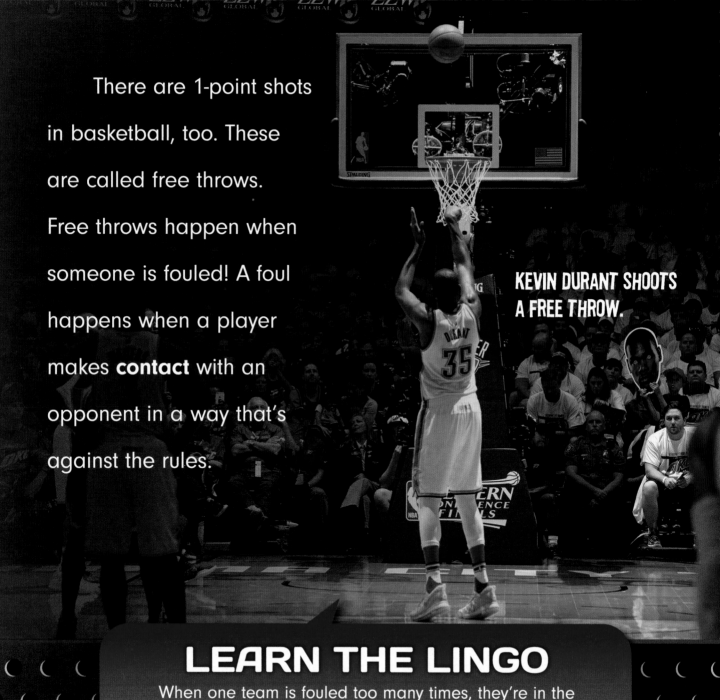

There are 1-point shots in basketball, too. These are called free throws. Free throws happen when someone is fouled! A foul happens when a player makes **contact** with an opponent in a way that's against the rules.

KEVIN DURANT SHOOTS A FREE THROW.

LEARN THE LINGO

When one team is fouled too many times, they're in the "bonus." They get extra free throws!

SHOOTING FREE

When a foul is **committed** against a player shooting, they get to shoot free throws. A foul on a normal field goal is worth two free throws. A foul on a 3-pointer gets three free throws!

HOME 08:29 GUEST

PERIOD 4

BONUS   POSS   BONUS

FOULS   SHOT CLOCK   FOULS

:17

SCOREBOARDS KEEP TRACK OF THE POINTS A TEAM HAS, AS WELL AS HOW MANY FOULS THEY'VE COMMITTED.

ON THE REBOUND

If a shot doesn't go in the net, the ball is up for grabs. Getting the ball off a missed shot is called a rebound. A rebound grabbed after the other team has taken a shot is called a defensive rebound. Grabbing your own team's missed shot is called an offensive rebound.

LEARN THE LINGO

A shot that goes in the hoop without touching the rim is sometimes called a "swish" because of the sound it makes! Some people say "nothing but net" because that's all the ball hits!

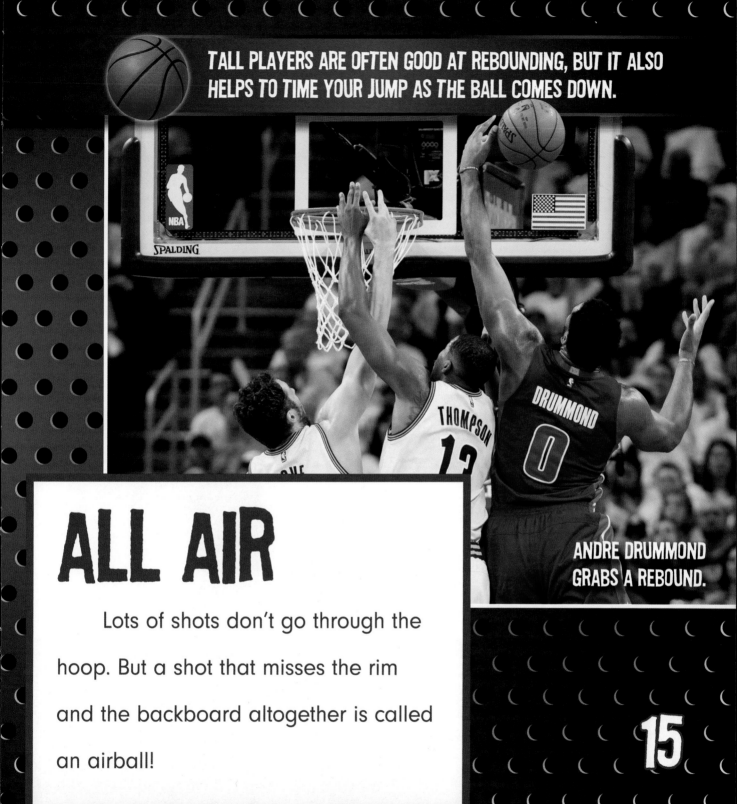

TALL PLAYERS ARE OFTEN GOOD AT REBOUNDING, BUT IT ALSO HELPS TO TIME YOUR JUMP AS THE BALL COMES DOWN.

ANDRE DRUMMOND GRABS A REBOUND.

ALL AIR

Lots of shots don't go through the hoop. But a shot that misses the rim and the backboard altogether is called an airball!

15

LINING UP

Other lines on the floor show different areas. The rectangular box under the hoop is called the key because it used to look like a key! The far end of the key is called the foul line. That's where players shoot from if they shoot free throws.

LEARN THE LINGO

A circle in the middle of the floor is used to start games. The ball is tossed in the air and a tall player from each team tries to tip it to a teammate. This is called a tip-off!

HIT THE BENCH

Players not in the game sit on a bench. That's where the coaches sit as well. Sometimes coaches will stand up and tell players what to do or where to go.

KEEP YOUR DRIBBLE

Once a player starts dribbling, they can start moving with the ball. If they stop dribbling, they have to stop moving. That's why "keeping your dribble" is important in basketball. If a player stops dribbling and starts up again, that's called a double dribble. Play stops, and the other team gets the ball.

LEARN THE LINGO

The foot left on the ground is called the pivot foot. It can't leave the floor, or you'll get called for traveling!

ONCE YOU TAKE ONE FOOT OFF THE FLOOR, YOU CAN'T CHANGE YOUR PIVOT FOOT. IT HAS TO STAY ON THE FLOOR, OR YOU'RE CALLED FOR TRAVELING.

LEBRON JAMES PIVOTS ON HIS RIGHT FOOT.

ONE FOOT, TWO FOOT

If you've lost your dribble, you can't move your feet anymore. You can still move one foot to try to find someone to pass to, though!

PASS IT HERE!

Giving the ball to another teammate is called a pass. Passing the ball lets another person dribble the ball up the floor and keeps the game going. There are different kinds of passes. The first is a bounce pass.

THERE ARE OTHER KINDS OF PASSES USED IN BASKETBALL, TOO. THROWING THE BALL OVER YOUR HEAD A LONG WAY, LIKE A FOOTBALL, IS CALLED A LOB PASS.

LEARN THE LINGO

Some great players can throw a pass one-handed or without looking where they're passing it! This is called a no-look pass.

USE YOUR CHEST

Another pass is called a chest pass. This is when a player pushes the ball away from their chest with two hands. The passer aims for the chest of the other player, too!

21

FIVE ON THE FLOOR

Each team has five players on the court at all times. These players need to work hard on both ends of the floor. Every basketball player needs to be good at offense and defense. When they're not trying to score points, players need to defend, or guard, their own basket!

THE FRONTCOURT

The frontcourt plays near the hoop. It's made up of the forwards and the center. The center works closest to the hoop. They're often the tallest person on the team.

LEARN THE LINGO

Most teams have two forwards—the power forward and the small forward. They often take shots from—and guard—the lower part of the court near the basket.

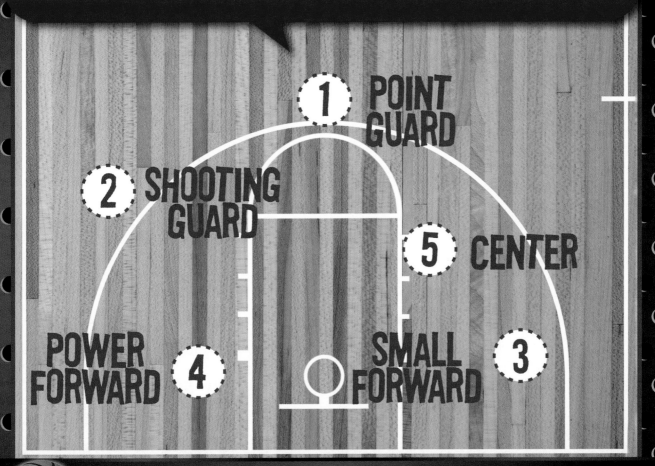

1 POINT GUARD

2 SHOOTING GUARD

5 CENTER

POWER FORWARD 4

SMALL FORWARD 3

HERE ARE THE BASIC POSITIONS IN BASKETBALL. SOMETIMES THEY'RE CALLED THE NUMBER THAT MATCHES THEIR POSITION.

Guards make up the backcourt of a basketball team. Guards work in the top half of the offensive zone, moving back and forth between the area behind and in front of the arc. Most teams have two guards—a point guard and a shooting guard.

◀ **RUSSELL WESTBROOK SHOOTS.**

POINT AND SHOOT

The point guard points, or leads, the offense. They have the best "handle," or ball handling and dribbling, on the team. They can also score, but often pass the ball to let teammates score.

LEARN THE LINGO

Shooting guards are often the best shooters on the team. They can score points from all over the floor—including behind the 3-point line.

STEPHEN CURRY PASSES THE BALL.

PASSING THE BALL TO A TEAMMATE JUST BEFORE THEY SCORE IS CALLED AN ASSIST.

25

TAKE A SHOT!

There are a few different ways you can shoot a field goal. The first is to take a jump shot. That's when you jump up off the ground and push the ball at the hoop with both hands. A lay-up is a shot taken close to the net with one hand. The ball often bounces off the backboard for an easy "lay" into the net.

CARMELO ANTHONY

SHOTS TAKEN CLOSER TO THE NET ARE OFTEN CALLED "HIGH PERCENTAGE" BECAUSE THEY'RE USUALLY MORE LIKELY TO GO IN.

THE DUNK

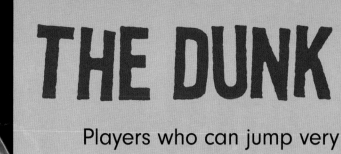

Players who can jump very high often slam the ball into the hoop. This is called a slam dunk!

DEANDRE JORDAN

LEARN THE LINGO

A shot taken when a player jumps away from the basket is called a "fade away." A one-handed shot in which a player hooks the ball over their head is called a skyhook!

MORE TO LEARN

There are lots of things to learn about basketball.

Coaches teach lots of different defenses and offenses.

There are lots of rules that cause **turnovers**, too. A steal is

when a player takes the ball away from the other team.

Different **statistics**, sometimes called stats, keep track

of points and other numbers to tell us how good players are.

LEARN THE LINGO

Triple-doubles don't happen that often, but quadruple-doubles almost never happen! That's when a player has four stats in double digits!

A player who scores double digits, 10 or more, in points and assists is said to have a double-double. If they also get 10 rebounds or steals, it's called a triple-double.

OSCAR ROBERTSON HAS THE MOST TRIPLE-DOUBLES EVER—181!

GLOSSARY

bounce: a springing back

commit: to do on purpose

contact: the meeting or touching of two or more things

determine: to decide

parallel: two lines laid in the same direction and always the same amount of space apart

professional: having to do with a job that someone does for a living

statistic: a number used to show a player's value in a sport

turnover: the act of giving the ball away to the other team in basketball

FOR MORE INFORMATION

BOOKS

Chandler, Matt. *Wacky Basketball Trivia: Fun Facts for Every Fan.* North Mankato, MN: Capstone Press, 2017.

Graubart, Norman D. *The Science of Basketball.* New York, NY: PowerKids Press, 2016.

Omoth, Tyler. *First Source to Basketball: Rules, Equipment, and Key Playing Tips.* North Mankato, MN: Capstone Press, 2016.

WEBSITES

Basketball Basics
hooptactics.com/Basketball_Basics
Learn more about basketball tactics and tips on this site.

Basketball Glossary and Terms
ducksters.com/sports/basketballglossary.php
Learn more basketball terms here.

NBA Video Rulebook
videorulebook.nba.com
Learn more about basketball's rules by watching videos here.

INDEX